Live At The

Freight House

February 21, 2018

by "johnmac the bard" & friends

1

"johnmac the bard" is a Trade Mark of **John F. McMullen** (a/k/a *"johnmac"* and, online, *"johnmac13"*).

ISBN: 978-0-692-10525-2

Table of Contents

4

Introduction

On February 21, 2018, I was honored to be the fourth "*Featured Poet*" at "*Poetry At The Old Put,*" a monthly series conceived by a young poet, **Christopher "Pinky" Gazeent**, and hosted at the historic **Freight House Café**, located in Mahopac, New York.

The Freight House Café (thefreighthousecafe.com), owned by **Donna Massaro** (*picture across page*) is set in the actual building of the freight house at the Mahopac station of the long-defunct Putnam Railroad line. It offers wonderful coffee, tea, hot chocolate, food, beer, wine, and martinis.

I had a rather dauting task as the fourth Featured Poet due to the talent and credentials of the first three:

- **Robert Milby – Poet Laureate of Orange County** and a well-known presence in the Hudson Valley
- **Tony Pena – Poet Laureate of Beacon, New York**
- **Bill Buschell** – Storyteller, poet, radio personality, and master of ceremonies at the **Hudson Valley Writers Center's** monthly Open Mic session.

The following collection contains the poems that I laid out to read (time considerations caused me to leave out a few), my notes on a few poems, the poems read by others at the Open Mic session that followed, their bios and a few pictures.

I extend heartfelt thanks to Donna and her staff for their hospitality, the audience which "packed the joint" for the event, "Pinky" for his foresight in envisioning the series, and, of course, **Barbara McMullen** for her support for the event, the production of this book, and in all other things.

What .. Where .. Why .. But

Audio-- https://johnmac13.podbean.com/e/what-where-why-but/

What?
- --- I read my poetry
- --- As often as I can
- --- Any place I find

Where?
- --- In Mahopac, NY
- --- In Stamford, CT
- --- In Sleepy Hollow, NY

Why?
- --- To practice my delivery
- --- To receive criticism
- --- To observe reaction

BUT
- --- I'm big
- --- have an even bigger ego
- ---- and have a temper
- --- So Shut Up and Listen!

Florida

Audio -- https://johnmac13.podbean.com/e/florida-1519085067/

Guns kill people!
People kill people!

It's guns!
It's mental health!

It's the school's fault
They knew!
It's the FBI's fault
It knew!

And we'll keep debating this
Until it happens again.

Background

I was an English Literature major at Iona College. Through a quirk of fate, I became a technologist and spent my whole business life as such. Not only did I not write any poetry for thirty-five years, I didn't read any.

Through another quirk of fate, I happened to pick up a book by **Charles Bukowski** in my local Barnes & Noble simply because of its odd title. I read one of his poems and thought *"This guy is off the wall – I could do this."* Shortly thereafter, I came across a quote in a motorcycle magazine that struck a chord with me and I wrote a poem about it, just for the heck of it.

One of my friends, **Jacqueline Birch**, looked at the poem and encouraged me to continue to write but I did not. Another friend, **George Hopkins**, encouraged me to enter the poem in a national contest and, while I didn't see the point, I did.

Four months later, he called to congratulate me in *"finishing third in the contest."* Although the prize was not overwhelming *($25.00, a year's subscription to "Poets & Writers Magazine" and online publication)*, it was an inspiration (*or a curse*) that led to hundreds more poems, four chapbooks, a 110-poem anthology, *"**New & Collected Poems by johnmac the bard,**"* designation as the **Poet Laureate of Yorktown, NY**, constant poetry readings around the Hudson Valley and Lower Connecticut, magazine submissions, poetry courses, and a general obsession with poetry.

The poem that started it all, *"**Cashing A Check,**"* follows.

Cashing A Check

Audio-- https://johnmac13.podbean.com/e/cashing-the-check/

I just saw this wonderful line
in a column in a motorcycle
magazine*:
"The mind writes checks that
the body can't cash".

The vision that many from the
old neighborhood have of me is
short and thin with a Pepsi in
one hand and a cigarette
in the other

Others will remember me as
taller and thin, hitting a jumper
from the corner or throwing
a "no-look pass" to a cutter.

Others will picture me at the
end of the bar in the Broadstone
with an open pack of Pall Malls and
a half-finished beer on the bar;
Don Gibson's "I Can't Stop Loving You"
on the jukebox.
"Pat, one more when you get a chance"

Age has taken the jumper
Diabetes has taken the Pepsi
Common Sense has taken the
cigarette and booze.

I am older and wiser and
hopefully more tolerant
I am satisfied with my life

but

to just be able to once more
fake the man guarding me and
go up with a jumper and
get nothing but net

To be able to, once more,
"cash that check"

*"Milestones" by Robert Rasor, American Motorcyclist; March
2006

How Do I Write Poetry?

Audio -- https://johnmac13.podbean.com/e/how-do-i-write-poetry/

When I started writing poetry
(after forty years of not
even reading poetry),
I just tried to regurgitate
all my thoughts and feelings.

Then I decided that to be really
professional as a poet,
I would have to know more
after the craft and the great crafters.

So I bought (and sometimes read)
poetry by Bukowski, Frost, Olds,
Field, Pound, Parker, Jong, Rich,
Berrigan (Ted and Dan), Collins,
Hughes (Langston and Ted), Corso,
Neruda, Rilke, Poe, Sexton, Plath,
Bishop, Angelou, Ginsberg, Auden,
Sandberg, Kerouac, Yeats, Stevens,
Noyes, and Hemmingway.

Some of them were very interesting,
some was even inspirational,
some was boring, and
some I even disliked.
But none of them were my voice.

So now, I sit and regurgitate
all my thoughts and feelings
and hope it has some value to
someone besides myself.
Maybe that's enough
... or maybe not.

Reality

Audio -- https://johnmac13.podbean.com/e/reality-1518106809/

Reading Billy Collins
or Bukowski
or Sharon Olds

Is like watching
Ted Williams hit
or
Steve Jobs sell a concept
or
Larry Bird see the court
or
Steven Hawking think.

I have aspired to
all these skills
and try my best.

But …

Poetry Readings

Audio -- https://johnmac13.podbean.com/e/poetry-readings-1517362287/

I read poetry
A lot now
—here—and
other places

At the conclusion
of each poem,
people smile and laugh
—even clap

When I finish all
the poems I read,
they do it again

This makes me
feel pretty good
—pretty good!

I'd feel really good
if they bought
the goddamn books!

Poem On Demand

Audio -- https://johnmac13.podbean.com/e/poem-on-demand/

We're sitting around talking about
an upcoming fiftieth anniversary party
and someone came up with the bright
idea that I should write a poem for the card.

What am I? Fucking Hallmark?
Would they have asked
Joyce Carol Oates to
dash off a short story?
or Stephen King to
come up with a short novel?

I didn't say any of this, of course.
I simply demurred –
"I do not do poems on demand"
but there was cajoling, asking,
and pressure until I capitulated.

So

Here's your fucking poem:
Happy Anniversary!

To Write A Poem

Audio -- https://johnmac13.podbean.com/e/to-write-a-poem/

I have to write a poem
for this new poets group.
Now what the fuck
am I going to wrote about?

How about sports?
Not enough folks may be interested.
How about sex?
Nah! Too personal!

How about politics?
No.
Some people in the group
may actually like Donald Trump.

How about …. Wait!
I already have 12 lines (14 now)
That's it.
That's my poem! Comments?

The Hudson Valley Writers Center
(writerscenter.org)

The Hudson Valley Writers Center, located in the Philipse Manor Railroad Station in Sleepy Hollow, NY is one of my favorite places. It has an unbelievably full catalog of courses, workshops, and seminars for writers of all genres and platforms. Additionally, on the third Friday of every month, there is an Open Mic in which writers (and other artists) get five (5) minutes to read or perform. I have been reading off and on there (mostly on) for almost a decade.

Snowy Night At The Writers Center

Audio - https://johnmac13.podbean.com/e/snowy-night-at-the-writers-center/

December 15, 2017

Travel warnings out
Snow in the road
I live 20 miles north
so common sense would say
"Stay Home!"

Yet, as usual,
I am the first one here
so I will be
the first to read.

As the starting time approaches,
there are only 17 others here
so it would seem that
wiser people have stayed home.

As the night progresses, however,
more and more arrive
and we learn, once again,
that writers are a crazy bunch.

"johnmac the bard"

Audio -- https://johnmac13.podbean.com/e/johnmac-the-bard/

I just bought a book of poetry,
"*In A Mirror Darkly*".
I enjoyed the poetry and it
was also illustrated very nicely.

I am rarely jealous of another's writing,
being of a sort who admires good work,
and I certainly don't envy the art
because I know it's something
I could never do.

What did bring out one of the
seven deadlies in me, however,
was the poet's name – his moniker
"Sullivan the Poet"

Damn!
That's a great name – and he grabbed it
before I thought of putting it on a business card.
(Not "Sullivan", you dimwit; "the Poet")

I told my wife of the envy
and she, as she oft does,
immediately had a solution
"You should be '**johnmac the bard**"

"johnmac the bard"? hmmm ...
I like the ring of that!
And it can tie into readings:
*"**Poetry Readings Tonight by
johnmac the bard**"*

Ok – print the business cards!

Three Poems

Audio -- https://johnmac13.podbean.com/e/three-poems/

I was reading my poetry tonight
at the Hudson Valley Writers Center
I had picked out three poems,
two brand new, one almost new.
The two brand new had been written
in the last four days,
one in response to Charlottesville and
the other a reflection on listening to other writers.
The third was from my recently published book,
"*33 poems Old & New*",
readily available for purchase
from Amazon.

When I got into the Writers Center,
I found that I had the printed pages for
the first two poems but that the book
containing the third was nowhere to be found.
What to do?
Although I had never recited one of my poems
from memory,
I decided to try, ad libbing when necessary.

It seemed to go well --
So well --
That I'll have to do it again,
when next the Sun rises in the west.

Submission

Audio -- https://johnmac13.podbean.com/e/submission-1517379107/

Dear Editor,

Enclosed are a few poems
which I sincerely hope
that you will choose to publish
in your fine journal.

In the event that you choose
not to do so, I hope that
your rag goes up in flames,
all your subscribers die, and
you and your staff rot in hell.

Respectfully submitted,
johnmac the bard

Goodness Gracious

Audio – https://johnmac13.podbean.com/e/goodness-gracious/

I saw him on television
this wizened old man
speaking softly
of days of yore.

And then the host
Don Imus, said,
somewhat cruelly,
I thought,
"Would you do a
song for us?"

As this little old man
shuffled toward the piano,
I thought "This is awful;
an affront to my memory
of a legend."

I was going to turn off
the television
so that my memories
would not be torn apart

And then the old man
sat down at the piano
and time reversed

The hands flew
the voice bellowed
and *"Great Balls Of Fire"*,
The Killer
Jerry Lee Lewis was back!

and so was I!

He Stepped Up

Audio -- https://johnmac13.podbean.com/e/he-stepped-up/

Wally Pipp was the first baseman
for the New York Yankees –
-- a good first baseman.
One day he had a headache
and asked the manager
"to put the rookie in today".
He did and Pipp never
started another game
for the Yankees
for the rookie
Lou Gehrig stepped up!

Chad Mitchell was the
lead singer of the
Chad Mitchell Trio
He left the group to
seek greater stardom
as a soloist.
You may have heard of his
replacement with the group
John Denver stepped up!

When the recently acquired
Bobby Thomson broke his leg
in spring training with the
Milwaukee Braves, it opened
the door for a rookie.
Henry Aaron stepped up!

When John The Baptist
lost his head, it was truly
a terrible thing
but the next guy
stepped up.

Up At 6AM

Audio -- https://johnmac13.podbean.com/e/up-at-6am/

Awake
I beat the clock
It won't go off until 7:30
I'll get an early start.

Up
Out of the bathroom
Now to make coffee
My Dunkin' Donuts favorite!

Whoa!
The clock says 2:45!
Alexa -- Temperature
6 Degrees!

So, it's freezing
And I'm up at 3 AM
I must be fucking nuts
I make the coffee.

Now, because I am up,
Fala, the Wonder Dog
and Ninja, the great black cat
Arrive -- Time to eat?

No way!
I finish my coffee
with Fala on my lap
All 12 lbs. of her.

I'm going back to bed
6 degrees at 3:15
Bah! Humbug!
Good night, everybody.

Ice On Lake Mahopac

Audio -- https://johnmac13.podbean.com/e/ice-on-lake-mahopac-1518907813/

Looking out from
the library window
No boats
No water skiers
No lake parties

Only Ice
and it is beautiful.

Spring will come
and all this will change.
Boats, skiers, and parties
and it will be beautiful too!

I Was A Basketball Whore

Audio -- https://johnmac13.podbean.com/e/i-was-a-basketball-whore/

I was a basketball whore
I played in the park
I played CYO ball
I played for an Episcopal Church
I played in a league at the Jewish Y

I played Intramural Ball in College
I was the proverbial "gym rat"
in college playing between classes
and often when I should have been in class
I went to Iona College,
I really majored in *"Basketball and Beechmont"*
The Beechmont is the bar across the street
from the college

Hey – I'm from Inwood
I grew up small and only grew late in college
I was a good ballplayer, then for a while,
a very good player, then a pretty good player,
then a good player again, and finally, an "OK player"
when I finally stopped in my mid '50s

I played in leagues on Wall Street
I played in "Open Leagues" around Manhattan and the Bronx
I played in leagues in Westchester
and -- "pickup" for two hours most Sunday mornings.

Now, I have regular cortisone shots in my hips and knees,
I've had minor surgery in both knees --
-- and then jelly pumped into them.
No cartilage in my knees or ankles and
arthritis all through my back, hips, knees and ankles
-- and my right ankle brings a limp and constant pain.
If the most recent shot and 24/7 brace doesn't work,
then it's fusion or a replacement – not a happy scenario

My orthopedist, an old player himself,
says that it's all from basketball.
If I had known then, back in my basketball days,
what I know now
I wouldn't have changed a fucking thing.

The Cane

Audio -- https://johnmac13.podbean.com/e/the-cane/

My father had a cane
that he used after knee
surgery for a torn cartilage.
I thought it was pretty cool.

Entertainers on television
sometimes used walking sticks.
I thought that
they were cool, too.

Over the years, I acquired
a number of hiking sticks and
Irish shillelaghs.
Also, very cool!

I got my own canes
after two surgeries
for torn meniscus.
I never had to use them.

But now, I have been
using one – a tall one --
because of pains in foot,
ankle, heel, and leg.

It is useful, primarily,
on stairs, hills, and
to lean on.
I hate the goddamn thing!

Perfection

Audio -- https://johnmac13.podbean.com/e/perfection-1518900527/

I do many things well
(if I may say so myself);
I even do some things very well
and I do some things not-so-well
(ask my wife).

But even for most of the things
that I do very well,
I do not do perfectly.

There is always something about
most efforts (even this poem)
that could be done better.

I know – because, at times,
I have done some things perfectly
-- well, at least one thing.

I have faked my defender,
dribbled into the corner,
turned and gone up in the air,
released --- and ---
gotten nothing but net!

As the ball drops through
and I start back down the court,
I know that there is nothing
that I could have done better
at that instant.

If only I could get that same
feeling from many more things.
Life is more than a jump shot.

Lucky, Not Proud

Audio -- https://johnmac13.podbean.com/e/lucky-not-proud/

I'm not proud to be an American;
being an American is not
an accomplishment of mine.
I didn't fight for its independence.
I didn't even choose to come here.
My grandparents did – and I will
be forever grateful to them
for their courage in coming here.

I am very lucky to have been
born an American.
I could have starved to death in Biafra,
been butchered in Cambodia,
gassed in Auschwitz,
sent to a gulag in Russia,
bombed in Hiroshima,
slaughtered in the Congo,
drowned in Indonesia,
blown up in Jerusalem,
or enslaved in the Sudan.
Instead, I was born in
the United States of America
and get to sit here and muse.

I am truly lucky as are my co-citizens.
Shouldn't we do whatever we can to ensure
that we don't have to be lucky not to be
starved, butchered, bombed, slaughtered,
drowned, blown up, or enslaved?
Or is it sufficient just to be jingoistic and
be proud of something we neither earned
nor even deserved?

Warning

If you're a fan of **President Donald Trump**, you might wish to skip the next three poems. I am not only not a fan – I have detested him for years before he emerged on the political scene. These poems are rather mild compared to what will be in my forthcoming Trump chapbook.

David Duke? David Duke?

Audio -- https://johnmac13.podbean.com/e/david-duke-david-duke/

In 2010, when asked about David Duke,
I, of course, knew who he was.
I'm not stupid!
In 2016, when asked about David Duke,
I didn't know who he was.
I'm not stupid!
Now people are comparing my comments,
even posting them side-by-side on TV!
Have they no respect for their President?

The Top Of My Hill

Audio— https://johnmac13.podbean.com/e/the-top-of-my-hill/

The top of my hill
in Mahopac, NY
is home to a "supposed State Park".
Supposed? Yes, supposed!

There are no trees in this state park
nor nature trails nor picnic tables
nor swimming pools nor fields
nor athletic fields or basketball courts.

The only path into the park is chained
to keep out the curious and
the misinformed who think there is a park.
It has been this way for years.

There is nothing there but overgrown weeds.
Big signs on the highway treat it as real;
driving by, you might be misled but
not the locals who know the truth.

This empty barren travesty of a state park
bears the name of our White House occupant.
Do you see a parallel here?

(Sign on Taconic State Parkway Photo – John F. McMullen)

(Picture from the State Park by John F. McMullen)

If You Walk With A Nazi

Audio -- https://johnmac13.podbean.com/e/if-you-walk-with-a-nazi/

The President of the United States
said that there were some "good people"
protesting in Charlottesville.
Not for the first time, he was dead wrong,

Good people may have showed up to protest
but, as soon as they stepped into the street
to march with people waving Nazi flags,
they were no longer good people.
The Nazis killed 8 million homosexuals,
gypsies, communists, and Christians,
and, of course, 8 million Jews
in their "Final Solution".
Over 400,000 Americans died in World War II
fighting Japanese Imperialism
and the murderous Nazi philosophy.
We saved the world!
Those who march under a Nazi flag
dishonor the "Greatest Generation"
and, unfortunately,
so does the President of the United States.

Blue Monday

Audio -- https://johnmac13.podbean.com/e/blue-monday-1507050837/

I woke up this morning
feeling really good,
after eight hours of sleep.
I made a cup of coffee.

I sat at the kitchen table
"Alexa News"
"Here's Your Flash Briefing"
"From NPR News"

"Live from NPR News,
this is Korva Coleman in Washington"
The top story – Las Vegas
40 dead at that time!
Shock!
Depression!
What could I do? No idea!
I had another cup of coffee.

58

Reverend Whackadoo

Audio -- https://johnmac13.podbean.com/e/reverend-whackadoo/

If anyone's religious sensibilities
will be offended by an attack
on the Reverend Pat Robertson,
he or she may leave the room.
This TV money grabber
blames "Lack of Respect for
Trump, the flag, and the anthem
for the Las Vegas carnage.
This is the same representative
of Jesus Christ on earth
who blamed gays and lesbians
for 9/11.
I prefer to think that it was
Stephen Paddock
and the plane hijackers
who killed all these people.

I do need God's help in understanding,
however, why people still send money
to this befuddled bigot who
demeans the message of Jesus Christ.

Creative Disruption

For years, I wrote columns on the hidden effects of technology on the world around us – the fact that we rarely notice the impact until someone in our family or neighbor loses a job or we finally notice that there are no more music (*eaten by iTunes*), film processing (*eaten by digital cameras*) or book (*eaten by Amazon*) stores in our local Mall.

The last extensive writing that I did on the subject were 122 weekly columns in series, entitled "*Creative Disruption,*" that ended when the newspaper in which it appeared went out of business.

The following poem relates to the ever-accelerating changes that sweep through our society, bringing consumer benefit, efficiency, and employment upheaval.

Who Do You Work For?

Audio -- https://johnmac13.podbean.com/e/who-do-you-work-for-1510950246/

Who do you work for?
That's sound like an easy question --
The answer may be for yourself
or for someone who gives you a paycheck.

But, if that is your only answer,
you just don't get it, cousin!
If you're like me and millions of others,
you work for a lot of people.

Let's see now.
I'm not sure I can list
all of the people that I work for.

I work for:
Amazon,
Walmart,
Home Depot,
Key Bank,
Con Edison,
and many more
that I can't think of
right now.

I order online,
check myself out,
pay bills online,
use ATMs.

I do so much
that used to be done
by employees of firms
but they are gone.

Banks that have teller
stations for six
have only two people
working now.

The people at Con Ed
who used to open envelopes,
take checks out,
input into systems,
and deposit into banks
are all gone.

I walk through my mall;
the film stores are gone
eaten by digital cameras;
the music stores have been
eaten by iTunes and Pandora.

Some of the many people
who have disappeared
have upgraded skills
and found better jobs.
Most have not.

For our employment,
by these vendors and
service organizations,
we have gotten convenience.

We no longer have to make
deposits in banks or
write checks or cart
computers and televisions
back from stores.

Things are much better
if you have another job
that feeds your life style.
If not?
Well, that's tough, isn't it?

My Inwood

Audio -- https://johnmac13.podbean.com/e/my-inwood/

I was born and raised
in the Inwood section
at the very top
of Manhattan Island.
It was an Irish Catholic /Jewish section then.
Each group thought that the neighborhood
belonged to them
and they were both right.

It had three claims to fame then:
a giant park with a large real forest,
Columbia University's football stadium,
and more bars than any neighborhood in NYC.
People came from all over to
watch football, play in the park, and drink in the bars.
Walter Winchell called it "GinWood"
in the press and on the radio.
The legal drinking age in NY was 18 then
so we could start in the park at 15 or 16.
When I first tasted beer, I didn't like it;
that soon changed!

We moved to the bars at 17 or 18.
Whether in the park or in the bars,
the beer was merely the catalyst;
it was the conversation that bonded us.
I no longer imbibe.
In the words of the great sportswriter Jimmy Cannon,
"*I stopped drinking twenty-five years ago;
I retired with the title*".
I knew a number who fell into the bottle;
most, however, did not.
We became engineers, lawyers, accountants,
writers, and technologists.

Were it not for half quart cans of Pabst
and the advent of the desktop computer,
I would never have become a writer.
So I owe a lot to the neighborhood and the culture.
I go back once a month for a luncheon.
There are now very few bars.
The neighborhood is Dominican at one end
and gentrified and expensive at the other.

The times and stores may be different
but the friendships and memories live on.
Inwood is now a "state of the mind"!
"*Who's got the church key?*"

The Traffic Survey

Audio -- <u>https://johnmac13.podbean.com/e/the-traffic-survey/</u>

Years ago,
over fifty to be exact,
I worked on
a Traffic Survey.

We stopped cars and
asked questions

"Where are you coming from?"
"Where are you going?"
"What is the purpose of your trip?

These are still good questions
--- for all of us.

Six Months Wonder

Audio -- https://johnmac13.podbean.com/e/six-months-wonder/

I was too young
for Korea
although I had a friend
whose older brother died there.

I was too old
for Vietnam
although I had friends
whose younger brothers died there.

I was working as a civilian
For the Department of the Army
and there was pressure to get my
"military obligation" out of the way.

So, I spent from November 1962
through May 1963 in Fort Dix, NJ
and Fort Sill, Oklahoma
as a six months wonder.

I hated it!
It was boring, repetitious and
an awful lot of "chickenshit".
I wanted to get on with my life!

It was only later that
I got to realize
how much I learned
in just those few months.

The Irish Catholic from NYC
worked with the Protestant
from Alabama who thought
that the Pope was a heretic.

The College English Major
found common ground
with high school dropouts
who thought reading was
a big waste of time.

The local basketball
gym rat and fanatic
found the same teamwork
as part of an artillery crew.

The kid from the lily-white
neighborhood of Inwood
saw his black platoon buddies
suffer bigotry and exclusion
in Lawton, OK.

The tedium of spit-shining
shoes and cleaning a rifle
with a toothbrush made
me "do things right".

It was only much later that I found
the answer to my constant question
"what is this 'good training' for?"
The answer was *"for life"*!

Pets

Audio -- https://johnmac13.podbean.com/e/pets-1510256885/

I don't know how people
particularly people
without children
live without pets.

Every morning,
I sit at the kitchen table
with my coffee and have
Alexa read me the news
(*Alexa is Amazon's home AI*).

Every morning, jet black Ninja
jumps up onto the table
and, then, onto my lap
for the ritual morning petting.

Ninja was a three-month old stray
who demanded to come into
our house and has brightened it
every day since.

Soon after, Fala the Wonder Dog,
a 12-pound Silky Terrier,
who thinks she is a Rottweiler,
barks for attention.

She is ready to arise and
be taken out. -- She doesn't
understand why, like Ninja,
she doesn't have indoor plumbing.

She is a Southern Girl --
-- a rescue from South Carolina
obtained when I found out that
her hair did not set off my allergy.

Later, when upstairs in a big office
where Barbara works,
Fluffy, a big gorgeous long haired
beige demands attention.

She was a local rescue
and has no desire to share her reign
with any vagrant
or southern princess.

Taken as a group,
although none of them
really like the others,
these are the best pets
we have ever had!

And – we have had plenty
to compare to – over 25 cats,
birds, hawk, tropical fish, ducks,
rabbits, a gerbil, and turtles
in 38 years.

Some were very bright or
affectionate or plain whacky;
most were great is some way
but, in total, none like these 3.

We feed outside animals --
-- deer, birds, squirrels, wild
cats, and a groundhog – it's
like giving back for the joy
that the indoor pets give to us.

Some say that they are
too old for pets;
It seems to me that pets
like these bring youth.

The looks of love that Fala
and Fluffy give to us is
heartwarming; Ninja's
flopping on our laps
brings peace and joy.

Ninja is lying on my lap
as I type now and it doesn't
get any better than this!

*Do you know this is
about you, baby?
I bet you do!*

Walking My Dog With Bad Wheels

Audio -- https://johnmac13.podbean.com/e/walking-my-dog-with-bad-wheels/

This doesn't mean that Fala has bad wheels
No, I do!
She can run and jump;
I can't.

No more going high for a rebound
or breaking out on a fast break
I used to leap and sprint
but now I hobble

Oh, well
It could be worse --
much worse
Many of my friends are dead!

Thirty-Eight Years Ago

Audio -- https://johnmac13.podbean.com/e/thirty-eight-years-ago-1518908125/

Thirty-eight years ago,
I had my last cigarette
Last year,
I was diagnosed with emphysema.

I started smoking
before the Surgeon General's warning.
It was adult then to smoke;
it was cool – like Bogart.

I believed "the doctors"
in white coats on television
who told me that
"Camels were good for my T-Zone"
(T in T-Zone meant both Throat and Taste)
I hope all those guys are dead.

Oh, well
I could have had lung cancer!

The First Born

Audio -- https://johnmac13.podbean.com/e/the-first-born/

Forty-eight years ago,
my daughter was born
with blue eyes
and a great smile.

I felt a rare joy
-- a different joy
one that only.
 came again
when my son was born.

She was a treasure
a pleasure
devoted to me
as I was to her
in short,
I stayed in the hospital
with her during operations
as a child and in college
I felt her terrible ear pain
when in Hilton Head

I watched her obsession
with school and running
and delighted in her many
victories and school records.

As a teenager, she was bright,
annoying, inquisitive, insecure,
smug, needful, strong
In short, a joy.

Then we got older
and something happened
I know not what
and we drifted apart.

I still remember the joy
of her clutching my hand
My first born.

Dedicated to Claire McMullen Cleary

On His 45th Birthday

Audio -- https://johnmac13.podbean.com/e/on-his-45th-birthday/

I smile when
I think of Luke,
my son Luke,
on his 45th birthday

While the rest of his family
father,
mother,
stepmother,
sister
wound up in different fields
than they entered after college.
Luke has followed his
grammar school dream.
He is a writer!
a television writer by trade;
his talent and interest took
him also into the writing
of adventure games.
More importantly,
he is the same person
at 45 that he was at 13.
a more mature person,
perhaps, but with the
imagination and presence
that he had as a teenager
when he

-- demonstrated computer games to 300
-- went twice to NASA's space camp
-- had published cartoons in Computer Shopper
-- travelled with us on business around the US
-- maintained friends around two separate homes
-- started a high school literary magazine
and, like his father,
failed high school geometry and
a foreign language because they
weren't on his crowded agenda
(again, like his father, his grades
ranged from outstanding to abysmal
while his mother, stepmother, and sister
were consistently around the top of the class).
Most importantly, he is interesting and a
pleasure to be around or talk to.
Since he was a child, he mixed seamlessly
with both adults and peers in two separate households.
and has retained the grace he showed then
When he was about 7,
he probably had a concussion,
jumping down stairs,
as Superman and
hitting his head on a radiator.
When he was in high school,
he definitely had a concussion
after being kicked in the head
in a soccer game.

38 years later
he is still
Superman
to me.
In case you haven't guessed,
I am very proud of
Luke John McMullen.
I just can't believe he's 45

Ode To Barbara McMullen
(on her **th birthday)
Audio -- https://johnmac13.podbean.com/e/ode-to-barbara-mcmullen/

Almost 40 years ago,
You and I, together,
left previous lives
and chose one of "us".

The choice was momentous,
ending corporate careers
and making our survival
dependent on each other.

We worked together.
travelled together,
cared for pets together,
and built a home together.

We built a business,
taught in colleges.
and wrote for publication.
The one constant has been us.

It hasn't always been easy;
We are both strong personalities
and we have argued –
often, heated and loud.

Yet, the joy has been great
and the love deep.
I would do it all again –
and again ... and again!

I am sorry for any hurt,
I thank you for every joy,
The 40 years have gone so fast
and I love you more than ever.

Mantra

Audio -- https://johnmac13.podbean.com/e/mantra-1517360441/

I am
Life is
We are
Let's keep it that way!

Backup

Audio -- https://johnmac13.podbean.com/e/backup-1517362036/

My Books are on my Kindle,
My Addresses are in my iPhone
My Calendar is in Google
and Gmail has my mail.

My writing is on my Pen-Drive,
My pictures are in Flickr,
My music is on the IPod
And my thoughts are on the Web.

All these are "backed up";
I am not
When my power goes out,
I do too

We Live To Die

Audio -- https://johnmac13.podbean.com/e/we-live-to-die/

We live to die;
this we cannot deny.

But we do deny
that we live to die.
We want to live
…to laugh
… to cry
…..to love
…...to fuck
……to read
…….to sing
……..to dance
………to learn

But, in the end,
what we have learned
is that we lived to die;
this we could not deny.

Why I Write

Audio -- https://johnmac13.podbean.com/e/why-i-write-1517363071/

I write prose to, hopefully, help others
understand what I understand --
the rigor of writing the prose also
helps me understand the subject better.

Poetry is very different!
I write poetry to help me
understand myself -- my feelings,
my relations with people and with the world.

I hope you like the poetry that I write--
but, if you don't, I really don't care.

Other Contributors

At the conclusion of my reading, the floor was opened to an "open mic" session in which other poets were able to read their poetry for a few minutes.

Following are the poems read by:

- **Carole Amato**
- **Vincent Bell**
- **"LC"**
- **Terry M. Dugan**
- **John Kaprielian**
- **Tony Pena**
- **Bob Zaslow**

and biographical information on each.

Carole Amato

Carole Amato holds Bachelor's and Master's Degrees from Mercy College in New York and has had careers in both the publishing and energy industries. She is an active member of the Mahopac Writers Group and both the Mahopac and Yorktown Poetry Workshops.

When We Lose Our Love

"If you love something, set it free. If it comes back, it will always be yours. If it never returns, it was never yours to begin with."

What happens when it doesn't come back depends on what your heart and mind did when it was with you
What you learned as you let it surround you
What you absorbed that you didn't discard
What seeped into your soul and remains as you face the world alone
What I now face without my teacher, my mentor, my friend ... my muse, my lover, my guide.

Which loss is deepest? I can't distinguish
There was a spark that my heart felt again after 30 years, like muscle memory
What caused the spark still instigates my heart when it wants to love
My fingers when they touch the keyboard
My eyes when they try to see the world and my brain when it tries to understand it.

This is not writing for writing's sake
These are words that spill from me like blood
As though a knife were thrust into my heart
Words that form in my mind become bloody beads on my forehead
As my fingers hover over the keyboard, trying to decide where to land that will not hurt.

But everywhere they land hurts
And every night, a million thoughts pour out of me as I wipe up
the bloody remains of my daily attempts to forget
Muscle memory, constantly pumping up my arteries
Spilling fresh blood each new day.

I've tried to harden my heart and let the blood congeal
But that damn spark will not go out, even as my blood washes over
it
And my heart refuses to become stone
Muscle memory ... forcing me to walk and talk and breathe.

Death

The words "No recovery can be made"
Hit like a bullet, caved in my chest
Not a soul I knew could have given aid
How could this happen? I had felt so blessed

Each ragged breath tore cruelly at my lungs
My pulse blew through me, ripping at my veins
My brain blathered as though speaking in tongues
There'd be nothing to bury, no remains

As in a dream, I knew not what to think
Living day by day waiting for the end
Faced with sink or swim, I about to sink
Saw vibrancy and bliss, become pretend

My dreams, now lost, I cannot rise above
Was not my body that gave out, it was his love

When Almond Trees Blossom

Oh look! An almond blossom on a tree,
 So beautiful, but only in the Spring;
Believe, believe, and miracles you'll see.

Fresh blossoms come to life so naturally,
Just once a year, a life for such a thing;
Oh look! An almond blossom on a tree.

For beauty men will go on bended knee,
The young in love may see a wedding ring;
Believe, believe, and miracles you'll see.

One Fall an almond bloomed unexpectedly,
The time was wrong, but it made my heart sing;
Oh look! An almond blossom on a tree.

None believed, they said no, it could not be,
But my heart soared like birds that take to wing;
Believe, believe, and miracles you'll see.

In autumn of my life love came to me,
A late new bloom, it now means everything.
Oh look! An almond blossom on a tree.
Believe, believe, and miracles you'll see.

Vincent Bell

I have been writing poetry for a very limited audience (mostly just myself) since I was a teenager. When I was still in college and graduate school, I tried unsuccessfully to get published - collecting a respectable number of rejection letters before giving up.

As a writer, I am interested in the mundane elements of everyday life. I work with them to ferret out simple complexities, ironies and hidden meanings. I strive for painfully sparse language by distilling my words so that they are simple and pure.

Ambulatory Delirium

The ones in purple are the orderlies,
the dark blue's are the nurses,
and the transporters are beige. The doctors'
scrubs are pale blue and shopworn. The floor's
pale white to help the cleaners see the stains.

The anesthesiologist interviews me
to hear my lies. "Are you comfortable?
Do you smoke? Recreational drugs?
Can you swallow? Eaten anything?
Loose teeth?"
It's always the hospital gown that breaks me;
the rest is easy. Foam swabs
on plastic sticks drip with mint disinfectant.
She hands me warm disposable
wash clothes for cleaning my belly — special
emphasis for my button. Can she see lint?

She's smiles like Vanna on Wheel of Fortune —
keeping it moving. Now I'm allowed some drugs.
Each step gets me closer to my scalpel.

Drinking Alone

I walked in to a bar and saw
Walt Whitman sitting there
staring into his drink.
He looked tired and past his prime.
His once impressive beard now
showed mottled gaps of skin.

He started one of those bar conversations
about sports and TV. After a few sentences
he said that he had been a poet,
but that he hadn't written anything recently.
I said that I was a poet
who was still writing and he said that he
felt sorry for me.

Walt said it was different
when he was younger.
He had freed American poets
from their own vestigial limits.
Other than editors,
poets don't have any
natural predators.
Their words flood the blank pages.

American Gulag

After Christmas, when
the hunted become hunters,
I see only dead trees
and Amazon boxes.
In our gulag,
I am a poet —
not a psychologist or a professor —
but simply a victim of nice chapbooks
filled with well-behaved poems.
We need more dive bar
stanzas about how clotty blood
flows in our streets.

The Trump Tube

After narrowly avoiding civil war,
elections were finally held for a new
president. Then Donald Trump
was placed in an iron lung
for the safety of the nation.
The new leaders thought that this
was a just punishment because
he couldn't play golf, grope women,
or reach his own penis.
The Trump Tube would allow
him to tweet with assistance;
and it would force him to breathe
while restricting all else.

LC

LC is the pseudonym for an anonymous member of the Mahopac Writers Group and the Mahopac and Yorktown Poetry Workshops.

A Soldier's Boots

I step into my boots
They carry me across unknown terrain
Fields clasped by tall, green, stalks
Arms, razor edge, slashing and humbling my every step
They carry me across a land of marsh
Where mosquitos, leaches and gnats lay in wait
Foraging, in their never-ending journey, for crimson drink
They carry me across hills cloaked with distorted trees
Through mist covered valleys with tangle brush and swift rivers
They softened my plunge from bird of battle
Onto the glebe field of choking stem and muck
That swallows my every step

The days, fiercely pounded—shrieks of lead and rocket
Yet my boots plow forward
Until I stumble
And touch the stiff of enemy
Is there a sign of breath, no—I'm sure
Then, I stride the red that runs beneath the twisted frame
In mind—there is only one way to go
Forward into the hate and pain
My boots steady me, I call for strength
Strength comes with each step
So casual does it flow
For now I know
It's only a game—I shout

When all is over
My boots take me to where I began
My melee has ended
With no more to endure
Nestled beside me, my boots
Now retired, they are in my service no more

Terry M Dugan

Terry M. Dugan's poetry confronts the devastating effects of war, epidemics and domestic violence on the people caught up by them. Since completing her MFA at Manhattanville College, she has won 10 awards for her poetry, fiction and essays. She has published poetry in many anthologies and she was invited to read her poetry at the United Nations, Hudson Valley Writers Center, Hudson Valley Museum of Contemporary Art, Hudson River Museum and her prose at Bowery Poetry Club and Bread and Roses Gallery.

The New Curriculum, February 15, 2018
The Day After the Parkland, Florida Shooting

Today's pop math quiz.
How many screaming students fit into
a classroom closet when the shooting starts?

Today's chemistry lab work.
What chemical cleans the blood
in the hallways, on computers, lockers, desks?

Today's phys ed drill.
How fast can you run when you see a gun,
how quick can you drop and roll?

Today's government and civics quiz.
If 90% of Americans shout gun control,
what percent of Congress will shut them down?

Today's health education test.
How do you perform CPR on a
kid bleeding from a AR-15 semi automatic?

Today's history question.
How soon will we forget your dead classmates and teachers,
remember the thoughts and prayers from political leeches?

John Kaprielian

John Kaprielian, a Russian linguist by training and employed as a photo editor for three decades, has been writing poetry for over thirty-five years; in 2012 he challenged himself to write a poem a day and in 2013 he self-published the 366 poems in a single volume, *366 Poems: My Year in Verse*. He lives in Putnam County NY with his wife and son and posts new poetry on his Facebook page https://www.facebook.com/366Poems/ and blog http://myyearinverse.blogspot.com/

Old Put

After the war
when my dad was a teen
trying to escape
the heat and
losing his father to cancer
he would take the train
the "Old Put"
up from The Bronx
on Fridays
with a bag and a
fishing rod
Getting off at Mahopac
crossing Route 6
climbing the hill to
Mary Avenue
where his uncle lived
in a house he built
from the cement he wheeled
from the lumber yard
across the street
and mixed with water
from the public well.

He'd lie in bed
and hear his uncle,
his "Amogli"
drumming on his headboard
and singing Armenian songs.
In the morning he would
take a rowboat
out on the lake
and fish around the islands
where the bass would lurk.
Alone on the water
he could
relax.

He always loved his time in Mahopac
but when we moved here
he never wanted to come and explore
the places in his past with me;
he stuck to the stories
and memories of the loving escape
he found there.

And on Sunday
he would grab his bag and pole
and the train
would take him back home
to his mother
and sister
and the quiet
empty
apartment.

Thaw

The icy wind that
sealed our lips and
bit our nostrils
is gone for now.

Fog hangs low over
the streams and lakes
providing a bit of modesty
as they change.

The soil animates our footfalls
with sodden squeaks and oozes
while worms below
awaken from their
dreams of decay.

Slowly at first
our chests expand
drawing in the warm, wet air

tentative

then a joyous rush
filling lungs and
displacing the
cold, dark, sad breath
of winter.

Rise up ye sleepers, awake!

In sleep, I glide past pools of blue
Astride by derricks tall and true
Ancient buttes and sacred lands
Torn apart by greedy hands.

(Rise up, ye sleepers, awake!)

I toss and turn while hillsides burn
Despite the smoke I can discern
The lines of people, dark and damp
Shuffling to detention camps.

(Rise up, ye sleepers, awake!)

In the streets self-driving cars
Carry us from work to bars
So we don't ever have to see
Faces unlike you and me.

(Rise up, ye sleepers, awake!)

We don't see all the misery
The toxic dumps and butchered trees
People bathed in sweat and racked with debt
While our "leaders" golf and joke and jet.

(Rise up, ye sleepers, awake!)

If this is what you want, you'll have it
Stay asleep, you'll never stop it
But rise and fight, for I hope this isn't
Your dream, your perfect future vision.

Tony Pena

Tony Pena was selected as 2017-2018 Poet Laureate for the city of Beacon, New York.

A new volume of poetry and flash fiction, "Blood and Beats and Rock n Roll," is available now at Amazon.

He also has a self published chapbook, "Opening night in Gehenna."

His publication credits include "Chronogram," "Dogzplot," "Gutter Eloquence," "Hudson Valley Transmitter," "Red Fez," "Slipstream," "Underground Voices," "Zygote in my Coffee," and others.

Colorful compositions and caterwauling with a couple of chords can be seen at:

www.youtube.com/tonypenapoetry
www.facebook.com/tonypenapoetry

A Smaller Set Of Balls

A nervous little nerd
I sucked in little league.
Skinnier than a Louisville
Slugger but with the speed
of a sloth and the hand
to eye coordination
of Jerry Lewis as
the Nutty Professor.
The opposing team made
me their unofficial mascot.
Got so bad my effigy
in uniform would hang
burning at the entrance
to the park where our team
boosters sold talismans
and garlic to neutralize me.

I was the Babe Ruth
of bad vibes, the Willie Mays
of the beaten like a dog
days of August with some
weird magnetic field around
me making baseballs
avoid my bat and glove
like the bubonic plague.
I prayed for rain the night
before every game but sure
enough the morning brought
sunshine and the butterflies
in my belly crashed against
the rattling cage of my ribs
desperate to fly off far away
from the fields of dreams.

When called upon to hit,
my team mates let out
a collective groan sounding
like a pride of hungry lions
at the Bronx Zoo and I
usually struck out swinging
like a runaway gyroscope
burning crop circles by
home plate unless I
was lucky enough
to get a base on balls
but the best was when
I got beaned on the skull
getting a smidgen
of sympathy for taking
one for the team.

But on the diamond
hope is a fly ball,
just ask Roy Hobbs,
and every once in a blue
moon the stars and planets
lined up just right
and the horsehide looked
like a beach ball in flight
and even my gangrened
glove caught the fucker
and all was right
with the world
and Annette's Buttons
until the next time
the lord of the flies,
Beelzebub, came to bat.

Buzzsaw

I slept with a wasp last night.
No, I'm not reliving 1977
barnstorming upstate
college town bars trolling
for femme fatales on
the fickle side of friendly.
This was an honest
to god badass bug.

A winged ninja assassin
surprisingly docile by my pillow.
Exotic eyes fawning over me
in a sweet and innocent
expression of buggy love.
Six long legs stretching
seductively as the alarm
goes off with Al Green
crooning , "Let's stay together,"
till my wife leans over,
her lips like valentines
quivering to Reverend Al
and all hell breaks loose
for as any fool will tell
hell hath no fury.

The wasp dive bombs us
till my wife runs out the door
screaming, "Kill that bitch!"
I picked up a People magazine
but she was buzzing by
with such unbridled passion
I knew light reading would not do.
So I rolled up a copy
of Poets and Writers,
jumping on the bed
en garding like Errol Flynn.

The wasp, jet black and sleek,
facing me in a stained t shirt
and plaid boxer shorts.
A Mexican stand off.
I thought I spied a sadness
in one of her eyes so
I thought of offering a truce
where I'd set her up
in a little hive just outside
the bedroom window.
We could spend plenty
of time together on the sly.
I searched her face
for a smile but found
only a sneer as she came
at me like Glenn Close
in "Fatal Attraction."

And I'm flailing away
like an epileptic Zorro
breaking two bulbs
on the ceiling fan,
perfume bottles flying
from the dresser,
picture frames falling
off the walls till I tripped
laying on the floor
defenseless till the door
opened giving way
to a floral scented fog
where my wife's silhouette
appears, her finger pressing
down on the button
of an aerosol can
like Senator Joe McCarthy
pushing the big red button
to annihilate the communists.
Gritting her teeth and scowling
in her best Clint Eastwood,
"nobody fucks
with the queen
of this house."

Bob Zaslow

I've been a teacher, a film-maker, an advertising copywriter, a playwright, a children's book author, a teacher again, a developmental literary editor, and most recently, a poet.

I've won a few awards for writing and an American Film Festival Bronze for a documentary film on a female artist, and one of my musical plays was selected for a short run at the FringeNYC Festival in 2011. I've also written and self-published and audio-recorded, ***Rap-Notes: Shakespeare's Greatest Hits***. (*Five of his most popular plays, in rap*)

And since the summer of 2017, I've been focused on moving from writing raps and rhymes to writing about more introspective things. Like what the heck am I supposed to be doing here? What's really important? And how can I touch people with words in a way that effects change?

In May, 2018, my wife, Ann, and I moved from our home on Lake Mahopac, New York, to a cabin on a lake in Bellingham, Washington. Smokey, our cat, lives here too.

Peace Piece

As a ruse, I photographed Bill Evans with my Nikon at the Top of
the Gate
And his jazzy notes were a jig-saw puzzle of harmony and discord,
impossible to hum
But they made me want to sing
Made me want to move inside and around them
Made me want to go to church go to heaven go to Rockaway
Beach in winter
And feel the music/cold/night pierce through me
I could hear his feelings like he was revealing them in black and
white
Which he was: 36 black and 52 white speaking parts
No structure no sequence no solutions no salutations no
cerebralizations
Just vibrations resonations actualizations ideations IDEATIONS
Without words or predictability, where expressions express
And we, the lucky audience, got to take it all in
If we also listened without words
Not like the rube talking up his girl while swirling the ice in his
Singapore Sling
And we got to hear what heaven probably sounds like
I heard it, I swear I heard it that day in 1970-something
On the corner of Bleecker and Thompson
And somewhere, up in my attic in a box, I've got photos in black
and white to prove it

Church at Auvers

I remember the first time a man-made object
took my breath away. I was twenty-two,
a young art teacher, traveling through Europe.
And as I rounded the grand stairs at the Musee D'Orsay,
I looked up, and saw Van Gogh's *Church at Auvers*.

I opened my mouth and felt my lungs fill with cobalt blue sky.
Forgetting I was in a museum, I shouted, "Oh, my God!"
I probably looked like some crazy American
tourist/eccentric/worshipper on that landing
because I stayed and stared perhaps thirty minutes
devouring every square-centimeter of canvas.
I took in the deep blue sky as though it were an animated movie.
And followed the wisps of clouds swirling behind the church,
which looked like it was carved out of purplish gray rock.
But, though bathed in afternoon light, emanated none of its own.
Could it symbolize the unenlightened? Empty preaching?
Then I dropped the questions. What did if matter?
No symbols, no symbols, not now.
Just the color and shape and form and flow;
the emotion in his brush strokes and how they made me feel.

Much later, I read Van Gogh's greatest wish was to show
what such a nobody as he had in his heart.
And when I read that passage, I flashed on the time in Paris
when I knew.
And for a moment, I felt my lungs fill again with cobalt blue sky.

Practice, Practice, Practice

A Japanese sage once wrote enlightenment is an accident
but spiritual practice can make you accident prone.
I laughed at his wit, then wondered what he meant.
I used to practice. On my guitar, on my flute, on my times' tables.
But spiritual practice...how do you practice on your spirituality?
Could I do that just by showing up in the moment?
And so, I imagined
what if I really tasted one raisin?
Really noticed how my fingers grasped this pencil?
Really smelled freshly crushed oregano?
Really listened?
Really felt my feet flattening down the grass?
Could I practice that?
Could the sage's practice be that simple?
That innocent?
Really?

Alchemy

I once watched a glass-blower at a Renaissance Faire.
And while his glob of glass was glowing
he transformed into a great alchemist,
changing the glob into anything--
a vase, a petal, a dragon.
It was pure potential as long as he kept it heated,
and spinning, and flowing like liquid fire.
And keep it heated, he did.

His face reflected the golden-white glow of the glob
as he spun and wove and danced and loved,
and showed the audience what it's like to be at one
with the fire, with creation, with pure movement,
and magical change upon change upon change.

But

once his ardor cooled
and his glass hardened
there was only one way he could change his creation.
Break it.

Dedications

In books, there are normally dedications to a few people for their support and/or help in producing the completed book. I must mention many more people than "a few" because the path to this book began long ago on Seaman Avenue in Inwood.

First and foremost are my family – my wife, **Barbara McMullen**, who has been unwavering in her support for the last 40 years and my children, **Claire McMullen Cleary** and **Luke McMullen**. My life was the product of the love of my parents, the late **Jack and Claire McMullen** and I was lucky to have for a brother (*and later a college teacher – two "A" grades and he threw me out of class once*), the best person I ever knew, the late **Robert McMullen**, whose own life was enhanced by his marriage to the late **Beatrice McMullen**.

I never would have made any commitment to poetry were it not for the encouragement of two friends, **Jacqueline Birch** and **George Hopkins**. Likewise, there would have been no "*Poetry at the Old Put*" were it not for the foresight of **Christopher "Pinky" Gazeent** and the hospitality of **Donna Massaro**, owner of the **Freight House Café**.

As mentioned above, my journey to get to this point was influenced by so many. The influence was not directly related to poetry – that would have been the furthest thing from our minds – but from friendships that supported both joy and intellectual curiosity and manifested itself in storytelling, often lubricated by beer. These friendships have stood the test of time although, sadly, many of the friends, such as **Mike Ryan**, my closest friend for years, **Bill McLoughlin**, **Bob Cummings**, **Joe Conway**, and **Bob Arco**, are no longer "with us".

I still have lunches and on-line conversations with friends from **Good Shepherd Grammar School, Cardinal Farley Military Academy, All Hallows High School**, and **Iona College** and, although I mention many names here, I am bound to have forgotten some that I should not have missed –but these come quickly to mind: my oldest friend, **Kevin Buckley**; my second oldest friend, **Gene Schneider** (*both were from my house, 254 Seaman Avenue*); my first grade friends, **Frank Mulderrig** and **Ed Winne**; my two-time best man, **Dan Sheehan**; my grammar school roommate, **Mike Cohalan**; my regular radio caller who has constantly reinvented himself, always to the better, in the 65 years that I have known him, **John "Chick" Donohue**; my friend of 70 years whom I am lucky enough to still see every week, **Jim Casey**; my neighborhood and Army buddy, **Warren Hennessey**; Inwood friends who have moved far away but remain in my thoughts, **John Valentine, Jim Connors**, and **Terry Sughrue**; two friends who are always there when you need them, **Denis O'Sullivan** and **Tom Hanlon**; the many great guests that have appeared on my radio show, including **Paul Levinson, Julie McCarthy, Mary Roach, Ralph Nazareth, & Sara Paretsky,** and the show's number one fan, **Therese Craine Bertsch**; the on-going members of the monthly **Inwood Luncheon**, particularly **Sandra Ward, Jim Finn**, and **Roberta McHale**; the founder and 20-year coordinator of the **Mahopac Writers Group, Vinny Dacquino**; members of the clergy who have impacted my life, **Bishop Jim McCarthy, Msgr. Tom Sandi, Mother Claire Woodley**, and the late **Dan Berrigan**; and so many more.

I thank the writers who contributed to this volume, the audience who came to hear us, members of the **Mahopac Writers Group** and **Hudson Valley Writers Center** who listen to my regular poetry readings, and to Yorktown Supervisors **Michael Grace** and **Ilan Gilbert** who have shown support for the Town Poet Laureate

.… and, once again, to **Barbara McMullen**.

John F. McMullen, *"johnmac the bard"* is the **Poet Laureate of the Town of Yorktown, NY**, the author of over 2,500 columns and articles and seven books, five of which are collections of poetry, and is the host of a weekly **Internet Radio Show** (*over 230 shows to date*). Links to the recordings of all radio shows as well as information on Poet Laureate activities and an event calendar are available at www.johnmac13.com. He is a member of the **Academy of American Poets, Poets & Writers, Hudson Valley Writers Center, Mahopac Poetry Workshop, Mahopac Writers Group**, and is the coordinator of the **Yorktown Poetry Workshop**.

He grew up in the **Inwood** section of Manhattan and lives with his wonderful wife, **Barbara McMullen**, in the hamlet of **Jefferson Valley, NY** and is the father of **Claire McMullen Cleary**, a physical trainer and life coach, and **Luke McMullen**, a television writer and video game writer.

Poet Laureate, Town of Yorktown, NY --
http://www.johnmac13.com/poet-laureate----yorktown-ny.html
Poets & Writers Site -- www.pw.org/content/john_f_mcmullen
In-depth Video Interview --
www.josephcarrabis.com/2018/03/07/john-f-mcmullen-johnmac-the-bard-a-life-in-verse/

130

Made in the USA
Lexington, KY
29 April 2018